Our Universe

The Moon

by Margaret J. Goldstein

Lerner Publications Company • Minneapolis

1391653l

Lerner Publications Company
A division of Lerner Publishing Group
241 First Avenue North
Minneapolis, MN 55401 USA

Website address: www.lernerbooks.com

Words in **bold type** are explained in a glossary on page 30.

Library of Congress Cataloging-in-Publication Data

Goldstein, Margaret J.
        The moon / by Margaret J. Goldstein.
            p.   cm. – (Our universe)
        Includes index.
        Summary: An introduction to the Moon, including its place in the solar system, movement in space, physical characteristics, and exploration by humans.
            ISBN: 0–8225–4658–2 (lib. bdg. : alk. paper)
            1. Moon–Juvenile literature. [1. Moon.]
        I. Title. II. Series.
        QB581 .G64 2003
        523.3–dc21   2002000310

Manufactured in the United States of America
1 2 3 4 5 6 – JR – 08 07 06 05 04 03

The photographs in this book are reproduced with permission from: © Roger Ressmeyer/Corbis, p. 3; NASA pp. 4, 9, 12, 13, 14, 17, 19, 21, 22, 23, 24, 25, 26. © Robin Scagell/Galaxypix.com, p. 15. © Arthur Morris/Visuals Unlimited, p. 11; © Hugh Rose/Visuals Unlimited, p. 27.

Cover: NASA.

It is nighttime. Stars shine in the sky. But something else glows bigger and brighter. What is it?

It is the Moon! The Moon is the closest
neighbor to Earth. It is closer to our
home planet than any other body in
space.

The Moon is much smaller than Earth.
Fifty Moons could fit inside our planet.

The Moon

Earth

The Moon **orbits** Earth. It travels around our planet. Earth orbits, too. It travels around the Sun. Eight other planets also orbit the Sun.

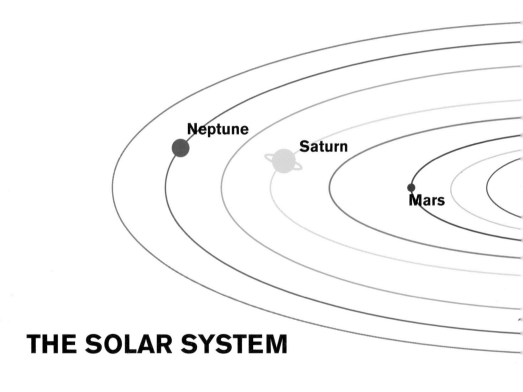

THE SOLAR SYSTEM

These planets make up the **solar system.** Some planets in the solar system have many moons. Earth has only one moon.

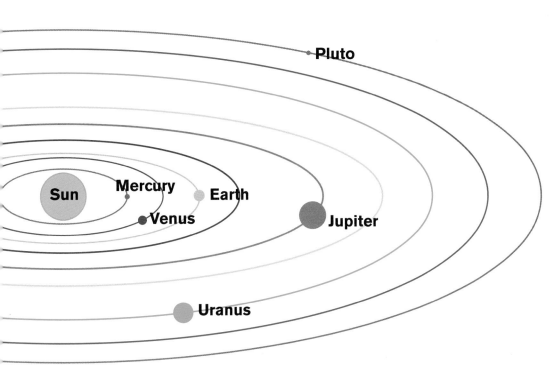

The Moon orbits all the way around Earth in about 27 days. The Moon moves in another way, too. It spins around like a top. The spinning is called **rotating.**

The Moon rotates slowly. It takes about 27 days to spin all the way around. It takes Earth only 1 day to rotate.

Earth

The Moon

The Moon does not make its own light.
Light from the Sun shines on the Moon.
The sunlight makes the Moon glow.

From Earth, the shape of the Moon
seems to change night after night.
These changes are called **phases.**

The Moon looks like a circle on some nights. Then it is called a full moon.

On other nights, the Moon looks like a
half circle. We call it a half moon.

The Moon can also look like the thin
edge of a circle. Then we call it a
crescent moon. Does the Moon really
change shape?

The Moon does not change at all. It is always a round ball. But each night we see different parts of it lit up by the Sun.

Phases of the Moon

The Moon is made up mostly of rock. It is covered by rocky gray dirt.

Tall mountains tower over parts of the Moon. Other places on the Moon are flat. These flat parts are called seas. But they have no water.

Billions of wide holes called **craters** dot the Moon. Some craters look like small pits. Others look like giant holes.

There is no life on the Moon. No plants or animals live there. There are no oceans or rivers. The Moon has no clouds or weather. It never rains or snows.

People could not live on the Moon. There is no water to drink or air to breathe. The Moon is very hot during the day and bitterly cold at night.

People from Earth have visited the
Moon. They are called **astronauts.**
Astronauts traveled to the Moon in
spacecraft.

Astronauts landed on the Moon for the first time on July 20, 1969. They came from the United States and traveled in a spacecraft called *Apollo 11.*

The astronauts brought tanks full of air so they could breathe. They wore special suits to protect them from hot and cold.

Astronauts on the Moon jumped from place to place. Their bodies felt very light. The Moon has less **gravity** than Earth has. Gravity is the force that pulls things toward the ground.

Other astronauts have visited the Moon since *Apollo 11.* Spacecraft have also visited the Moon without astronauts. These spacecraft carried machines to collect information.

Look up into the night sky. What would you do if you could visit the Moon?

Facts about the Moon

- The Moon is 239,000 miles (384,000 km) from Earth.

- The Moon's diameter (distance across) is 2,160 miles (3,480 km).

- The Moon orbits Earth in 27 days.

- The Moon rotates in 27 days.

- The Moon's average daytime temperature is 225°F (107°C).

- The Moon's average nighttime temperature is −243°F (−153°C).

- The Moon has been visited by many American missions, including the *Pioneer* program in 1958–1959, the *Ranger* program in 1961–1965, the *Surveyor* program in 1966–1968, the *Lunar Orbiter* program in 1966–1967, the *Apollo* program in 1968–1972,

Clementine in 1994, and *Lunar Prospector* in 1998–1999.

- One side of the Moon always faces away from Earth. It is called the dark side of the Moon. A spacecraft took the first pictures of the dark side in 1959.

- There is no wind on the Moon. Astronauts used wire to make the American flag on the Moon stiff. It looks like it is flying in the wind.

- People standing on the Moon weigh only one-sixth of what they weigh on Earth. If you weigh 60 pounds on Earth, you would weigh only 10 pounds on the Moon.

- More than 70 spacecraft have visited the Moon. Twelve astronauts have walked on the Moon. Neil Armstrong and Buzz Aldrin were the first astronauts to walk on the Moon.

Glossary

astronaut: a person who travels into space

crater: a large hole on a moon or planet

crescent: the thin curved edge of a circle

gravity: a force that pulls objects toward the Sun, planets, or moons

orbit: to travel around a larger body in space

phases: the changes we see in the Moon from night to night

rotate: to spin around

solar system: the Sun and the planets, moons, and other objects that travel around it

Learn More about the Moon

Books
Furniss, Tim. *The Moon.* Austin, TX: Raintree Steck-Vaughn, 2000.

Gibbons, Gail. *The Moon Book.* New York: Holiday House, 1997.

Simon, Seymour. *The Moon.* New York: Simon and Schuster, 1984.

Websites
Solar System Exploration: The Moon
<http://solarsystem.nasa.gov/features/planets/moon/moon.html>
Detailed information from the National Aeronautics and Space
Administration (NASA) about the Moon, with good links to other
helpful websites.

The Space Place
<http://spaceplace.jpl.nasa.gov>
An astronomy website for kids developed by the Jet Propulsion
Laboratory.

StarChild
http://starchild.gsfc.nasa.gov/docs/StarChild/StarChild.html>
An online learning center for young astronomers, sponsored by
NASA.

Index